Enjoy Mathematics Series – book four

Practice Examples in Basic Division

John and Patricia Moore

POND VIEW BOOKS

Revised Edition 2005
© Forward Press Limited 2005

ISBN 1-871044-10-3

Printed in Great Britain by Forward Press Limited

Published by
Pond View, Remus House, Coltsfoot Drive,
Woodston, Peterborough, PE2 9JX

Foreword

This is not a teaching scheme, but sets of exercises for the use of Primary School pupils, and pupils in Secondary Schools in need of revision in basic mathematics.

No attempt has been made to suggest methods for working. There is often more than one perfectly legitimate way of obtaining the correct answer. We do not believe that slower pupils should be confused by being confronted with a different method from the one used by their teacher. Very carefully graded material is used, with correct development of steps, introducing one difficulty at a time.

In the early material on Addition and Subtraction, great emphasis has been placed on the number bond 10 (1+ 9 = 10, 2 + 8 = 10, etc). This is included in almost every example.

In Subtraction, some children find it extremely difficult to subtract from 0. This may be laziness, but frequently they have had little grounding in 'making up to 10'. They need, therefore, much practice to cope with this particular difficulty. For this reason, we do not apologise for repetition in basic processes.

In the books dealing with Multiplication and Division, digits have been repeated many times to reinforce learning the table. The table square is included inside the Multiplication front cover. It is always available for reference, if needed.

In Division by divisors up to 12, care has been taken to use the simplest carrying figures in the early stages, gradually increasing in difficulty by very easy steps. Long division has been included, although it is not now popular with many teachers, or included in many schemes. This, in our experience, can be taught with greater ease if the units digit is 1 in the divisor. It is easier to divide by 91 than by 19. The first stage, therefore, is division by 21, 31, 41, etc, and then increasing the units digit by easy stages to 22, 32, 42, etc, and 23, 33, 43, etc. It is also valuable to have the multiplication table of the divisor written out, and this we have asked the pupils to do. In our opinion, long division is worthy of more attention, as it gives practice in subtraction and multiplication, as well as division.

We have used large type, and a clear, distinct format for our exercises.

Children who are not given prepared columns to work with initially are inclined to ignore the fact that columns are required, and squash all the numbers together.

How the book is used is left entirely to the discretion of the teacher, who knows the needs of particular individuals. Even in a small Remedial Unit there will be pupils of varying abilities, with very different weaknesses. Less able pupils need to have evidence of progress, even if it is slow. The work has to be arranged so that the end of an exercise is always in sight, and attainable.

In examples involving problems, the language used has been kept very simple, so that difficulties with reading will not hamper arithmetical attainment.

We hope that the very carefully graded exercises in these books will be to the mutual advantage of teachers and their pupils in the quest for high standards of numeracy.

John and Patricia Moore

Contents

Exercises D1–D2   Division of numbers up to 120, involving no carrying figure, or a carrying figure of 1. No remainders.

Exercises D3–D4   Division of tens and units by a single digit. Simple carrying figure. Some remainders.

Exercises D5–D9   Division of hundreds, tens and units by 2, 3, 4, 5 and 6.

Exercises D10–D11   Division of hundreds, tens and units by 7 and 8.

Exercises D12–D14   Harder examples of division of hundreds, tens and units, some with remainders.

Exercises D15–D17   Division of thousands, hundreds, tens and units by numbers less than 10.

Exercises D18–D23   Division of 5-digit numbers by numbers up to 12, with remainders.

Exercises D24–D27   Division by 21, first completing 21-times table.

Exercises D28–D34   Division by 31, 41, 51, 61, 71 and 81, involving two operations. Appropriate table to be completed before each exercise.

Exercises D35–D40   Division by 32, 42, 52, 62, 72 and 82, involving two operations. Appropriate table to be completed before each exercise.

Exercises D41–D45   Division by 43, 54, 65, 75 and 87, involving two operations. Appropriate table to be completed before each exercise.

Exercises D46–D51   Harder examples of division by numbers from 45–98, using two or three operations.

Exercises D52–D54   Examples using the alternative division sign.

Exercises D55–D58   Simple problems.

Exercises D59–D62   Cross-number puzzles.

Exercise D1

a. $2\overline{)24}$ b. $2\overline{)28}$ c. $2\overline{)26}$ d. $2\overline{)22}$

e. $3\overline{)30}$ f. $3\overline{)33}$ g. $3\overline{)36}$ h. $3\overline{)39}$

i. $4\overline{)40}$ j. $4\overline{)44}$ k. $4\overline{)48}$ l. $5\overline{)50}$

m. $5\overline{)55}$ n. $6\overline{)60}$ o. $6\overline{)66}$ p. $7\overline{)70}$

q. $7\overline{)77}$ r. $8\overline{)80}$ s. $9\overline{)90}$ t. $8\overline{)88}$

u. $9\overline{)99}$ v. $10\overline{)100}$ w. $11\overline{)110}$ x. $12\overline{)120}$

Exercise D2

a. $2\overline{)42}$　　b. $3\overline{)60}$　　c. $3\overline{)66}$　　d. $2\overline{)84}$

e. $4\overline{)80}$　　f. $2\overline{)86}$　　g. $2\overline{)44}$　　h. $2\overline{)46}$

i. $3\overline{)69}$　　j. $2\overline{)36}$　　k. $2\overline{)66}$　　l. $2\overline{)88}$

m. $3\overline{)63}$　　n. $2\overline{)64}$　　o. $4\overline{)84}$　　p. $2\overline{)82}$

q. $2\overline{)48}$　　r. $2\overline{)62}$　　s. $4\overline{)88}$　　t. $2\overline{)38}$

u. $2\overline{)60}$　　v. $2\overline{)30}$　　w. $2\overline{)34}$　　x. $2\overline{)32}$

Exercise D3

a. $3\overline{)42}$ b. $6\overline{)72}$ c. $5\overline{)65}$ d. $3\overline{)54}$

e. $3\overline{)57}$ f. $4\overline{)52}$ g. $3\overline{)51}$ h. $4\overline{)68}$

i. $4\overline{)60}$ j. $5\overline{)70}$ k. $6\overline{)78}$ l. $4\overline{)56}$

m. $3\overline{)45}$ n. $4\overline{)64}$ o. $4\overline{)72}$ p. $3\overline{)48}$

q. $5\overline{)75}$ r. $7\overline{)98}$ s. $6\overline{)84}$ t. $6\overline{)90}$

u. $8\overline{)96}$ v. $7\overline{)84}$ w. $7\overline{)91}$ x. $5\overline{)85}$

Exercise D4

a. $2\overline{)35}$ b. $2\overline{)37}$ c. $2\overline{)33}$ d. $2\overline{)39}$

e. $3\overline{)34}$ f. $3\overline{)35}$ g. $3\overline{)37}$ h. $4\overline{)45}$

i. $5\overline{)56}$ j. $6\overline{)67}$ k. $7\overline{)78}$ l. $8\overline{)89}$

m. $3\overline{)49}$ n. $3\overline{)52}$ o. $3\overline{)58}$ p. $3\overline{)56}$

q. $4\overline{)58}$ r. $4\overline{)65}$ s. $5\overline{)76}$ t. $4\overline{)69}$

u. $5\overline{)78}$ v. $5\overline{)79}$ w. $6\overline{)87}$ x. $6\overline{)89}$

Exercise D5

a. $2\overline{)338}$ b. $2\overline{)336}$ c. $2\overline{)358}$

d. $2\overline{)374}$ e. $2\overline{)354}$ f. $2\overline{)396}$

g. $2\overline{)376}$ h. $2\overline{)392}$ i. $2\overline{)574}$

j. $2\overline{)596}$ k. $2\overline{)534}$ l. $2\overline{)556}$

m. $2\overline{)590}$ n. $2\overline{)552}$ o. $2\overline{)574}$

p. $2\overline{)774}$ q. $2\overline{)736}$ r. $2\overline{)752}$

s. $2\overline{)750}$ t. $2\overline{)712}$ u. $2\overline{)756}$

v. $2\overline{)792}$ w. $2\overline{)732}$ x. $2\overline{)976}$

Exercise D6

a. 3⟌474

b. 3⟌492

c. 3⟌411

d. 3⟌474

e. 3⟌465

f. 3⟌468

g. 3⟌432

h. 3⟌447

i. 3⟌552

j. 3⟌714

k. 3⟌738

l. 3⟌753

m. 3⟌771

n. 3⟌792

o. 3⟌768

p. 3⟌702

q. 3⟌717

r. 3⟌591

s. 3⟌546

t. 3⟌561

u. 3⟌582

v. 3⟌588

w. 3⟌504

x. 3⟌507

Exercise D7

a. $4\overline{)576}$ b. $4\overline{)596}$ c. $4\overline{)536}$

d. $4\overline{)584}$ e. $4\overline{)504}$ f. $4\overline{)508}$

g. $4\overline{)516}$ h. $4\overline{)552}$ i. $4\overline{)616}$

j. $4\overline{)632}$ k. $4\overline{)696}$ l. $4\overline{)652}$

m. $4\overline{)692}$ n. $4\overline{)676}$ o. $4\overline{)636}$

p. $4\overline{)612}$ q. $4\overline{)772}$ r. $4\overline{)792}$

s. $4\overline{)732}$ t. $4\overline{)704}$ u. $4\overline{)736}$

v. $4\overline{)756}$ w. $4\overline{)776}$ x. $4\overline{)780}$

Exercise D8

a. 5⟌675

b. 5⟌635

c. 5⟌685

d. 5⟌690

e. 5⟌630

f. 5⟌645

g. 5⟌615

h. 5⟌625

i. 5⟌740

j. 5⟌765

k. 5⟌720

l. 5⟌790

m. 5⟌710

n. 5⟌780

o. 5⟌725

p. 5⟌765

q. 5⟌845

r. 5⟌865

s. 5⟌885

t. 5⟌875

u. 5⟌860

v. 5⟌815

w. 5⟌855

x. 5⟌890

Exercise D9

a. 6⟌738

b. 6⟌744

c. 6⟌756

d. 6⟌762

e. 6⟌732

f. 6⟌768

g. 6⟌774

h. 6⟌858

i. 6⟌828

j. 6⟌864

k. 6⟌894

l. 6⟌870

m. 6⟌888

n. 6⟌816

o. 6⟌834

p. 6⟌978

q. 6⟌918

r. 6⟌924

s. 6⟌990

t. 6⟌984

u. 6⟌972

v. 6⟌936

w. 6⟌948

x. 6⟌768

Exercise D10

a. $7\overline{)826}$ b. $7\overline{)833}$ c. $7\overline{)854}$

d. $7\overline{)875}$ e. $7\overline{)812}$ f. $7\overline{)889}$

g. $7\overline{)861}$ h. $7\overline{)896}$ i. $7\overline{)924}$

j. $7\overline{)938}$ k. $7\overline{)966}$ l. $7\overline{)945}$

m. $7\overline{)994}$ n. $7\overline{)959}$ o. $7\overline{)973}$

p. $7\overline{)980}$ q. $7\overline{)840}$ r. $7\overline{)868}$

s. $7\overline{)882}$ t. $7\overline{)903}$ u. $7\overline{)861}$

v. $7\overline{)917}$ w. $7\overline{)931}$ x. $7\overline{)952}$

Exercise D11

a. 8 ⟌ 9 1 2   b. 8 ⟌ 9 2 8   c. 8 ⟌ 9 4 4

d. 8 ⟌ 9 8 4   e. 8 ⟌ 8 1 6   f. 8 ⟌ 9 0 4

g. 8 ⟌ 9 3 6   h. 8 ⟌ 9 9 2   i. 8 ⟌ 8 3 2

j. 8 ⟌ 8 7 2   k. 8 ⟌ 9 7 6   l. 8 ⟌ 8 5 6

m. 8 ⟌ 9 6 8   n. 8 ⟌ 8 6 4   o. 8 ⟌ 8 0 8

p. 8 ⟌ 9 6 0   q. 8 ⟌ 8 9 6   r. 8 ⟌ 8 4 0

s. 8 ⟌ 9 5 2   t. 8 ⟌ 7 9 2   u. 8 ⟌ 8 8 0

v. 8 ⟌ 8 4 8   w. 8 ⟌ 8 8 8   x. 8 ⟌ 8 2 4

Exercise D12

a. $2\overline{)178}$　　　　b. $2\overline{)196}$　　　　c. $2\overline{)156}$

d. $2\overline{)198}$　　　　e. $3\overline{)291}$　　　　f. $3\overline{)261}$

g. $3\overline{)282}$　　　　h. $3\overline{)255}$　　　　i. $4\overline{)332}$

j. $4\overline{)344}$　　　　k. $4\overline{)356}$　　　　l. $4\overline{)392}$

m. $5\overline{)465}$　　　　n. $5\overline{)475}$　　　　o. $5\overline{)495}$

p. $5\overline{)485}$　　　　q. $6\overline{)588}$　　　　r. $6\overline{)522}$

s. $6\overline{)564}$　　　　t. $6\overline{)576}$　　　　u. $7\overline{)644}$

v. $7\overline{)651}$　　　　w. $7\overline{)686}$　　　　x. $7\overline{)693}$

Exercise D13

a. $2 \overline{)154}$ b. $3 \overline{)261}$ c. $4 \overline{)364}$

d. $5 \overline{)470}$ e. $4 \overline{)372}$ f. $3 \overline{)273}$

g. $5 \overline{)455}$ h. $2 \overline{)188}$ i. $5 \overline{)425}$

j. $6 \overline{)534}$ k. $9 \overline{)648}$ l. $9 \overline{)684}$

m. $9 \overline{)657}$ n. $9 \overline{)693}$ o. $9 \overline{)675}$

p. $8 \overline{)736}$ q. $9 \overline{)846}$ r. $9 \overline{)873}$

s. $8 \overline{)776}$ t. $9 \overline{)702}$ u. $9 \overline{)855}$

v. $8 \overline{)752}$ w. $9 \overline{)666}$ x. $9 \overline{)891}$

Exercise D14

a. $2\overline{)161}$ b. $2\overline{)191}$ c. $3\overline{)211}$

d. $3\overline{)241}$ e. $4\overline{)323}$ f. $4\overline{)362}$

g. $4\overline{)243}$ h. $4\overline{)281}$ i. $5\overline{)454}$

j. $5\overline{)253}$ k. $5\overline{)352}$ l. $5\overline{)302}$

m. $6\overline{)364}$ n. $6\overline{)424}$ o. $6\overline{)543}$

p. $6\overline{)501}$ q. $7\overline{)493}$ r. $7\overline{)634}$

s. $7\overline{)492}$ t. $7\overline{)563}$ u. $8\overline{)564}$

v. $8\overline{)325}$ w. $8\overline{)724}$ x. $8\overline{)242}$

Exercise D15

a. $2\overline{)3187}$ b. $2\overline{)5795}$ c. $2\overline{)7956}$

d. $3\overline{)4972}$ e. $3\overline{)5784}$ f. $3\overline{)8543}$

g. $4\overline{)6984}$ h. $4\overline{)7946}$ i. $4\overline{)9854}$

j. $5\overline{)7946}$ k. $5\overline{)8462}$ l. $5\overline{)7427}$

m. $6\overline{)7865}$ n. $6\overline{)8590}$ o. $6\overline{)9374}$

p. $7\overline{)8426}$ q. $7\overline{)9486}$ r. $7\overline{)8657}$

s. $8\overline{)9946}$ t. $8\overline{)9764}$ u. $8\overline{)9999}$

v. $5\overline{)6239}$ w. $4\overline{)9867}$ x. $5\overline{)9506}$

Exercise D16

a. $2\overline{)1164}$ b. $2\overline{)1784}$ c. $2\overline{)1796}$

d. $3\overline{)1964}$ e. $3\overline{)2974}$ f. $3\overline{)2846}$

g. $4\overline{)2865}$ h. $4\overline{)1896}$ i. $4\overline{)3564}$

j. $5\overline{)2765}$ k. $5\overline{)3876}$ l. $5\overline{)4957}$

m. $6\overline{)3748}$ n. $6\overline{)4869}$ o. $6\overline{)5892}$

p. $7\overline{)3894}$ q. $7\overline{)4864}$ r. $7\overline{)5776}$

s. $8\overline{)5934}$ t. $8\overline{)6984}$ u. $8\overline{)7762}$

v. $9\overline{)6743}$ w. $9\overline{)7567}$ x. $9\overline{)8994}$

Exercise D17

a. $2\overline{)1605}$ b. $2\overline{)1807}$ c. $2\overline{)1401}$

d. $3\overline{)2107}$ e. $3\overline{)2705}$ f. $3\overline{)2402}$

g. $4\overline{)3209}$ h. $4\overline{)3607}$ i. $4\overline{)2403}$

j. $5\overline{)4509}$ k. $5\overline{)3508}$ l. $5\overline{)2502}$

m. $6\overline{)3607}$ n. $6\overline{)4208}$ o. $6\overline{)4805}$

p. $7\overline{)4907}$ q. $7\overline{)5608}$ r. $7\overline{)6303}$

s. $8\overline{)7204}$ t. $8\overline{)6409}$ u. $8\overline{)6408}$

v. $9\overline{)1804}$ w. $9\overline{)7206}$ x. $9\overline{)8108}$

Exercise D18

a. $2\overline{)37208}$

b. $2\overline{)58604}$

c. $2\overline{)99207}$

d. $3\overline{)89104}$

e. $3\overline{)73205}$

f. $3\overline{)52202}$

g. $4\overline{)57207}$

h. $4\overline{)65605}$

i. $4\overline{)93402}$

j. $5\overline{)65505}$

k. $5\overline{)72508}$

l. $5\overline{)85002}$

m. $6\overline{)73202}$

n. $6\overline{)85307}$

o. $6\overline{)97206}$

p. $7\overline{)85406}$

q. $7\overline{)89607}$

r. $7\overline{)84009}$

s. $8\overline{)98401}$

t. $8\overline{)91408}$

Exercise D19

a. $2 \overline{)19801}$

b. $2 \overline{)17605}$

c. $2 \overline{)19200}$

d. $3 \overline{)28201}$

e. $3 \overline{)19203}$

f. $3 \overline{)20408}$

g. $4 \overline{)33203}$

h. $4 \overline{)29206}$

i. $4 \overline{)37202}$

j. $5 \overline{)46505}$

k. $5 \overline{)38502}$

l. $5 \overline{)47010}$

m. $6 \overline{)52802}$

n. $6 \overline{)37209}$

o. $6 \overline{)39005}$

p. $7 \overline{)64403}$

q. $7 \overline{)37108}$

r. $7 \overline{)59500}$

s. $8 \overline{)66403}$

t. $8 \overline{)78409}$

Exercise D20

a. $8\overline{\smash{\big)}99645}$

b. $8\overline{\smash{\big)}79216}$

c. $9\overline{\smash{\big)}89676}$

d. $9\overline{\smash{\big)}86764}$

e. $7\overline{\smash{\big)}50546}$

f. $8\overline{\smash{\big)}67217}$

g. $7\overline{\smash{\big)}50669}$

h. $8\overline{\smash{\big)}66570}$

i. $9\overline{\smash{\big)}39086}$

j. $8\overline{\smash{\big)}17986}$

k. $9\overline{\smash{\big)}59094}$

l. $8\overline{\smash{\big)}99946}$

m. $8\overline{\smash{\big)}49986}$

n. $8\overline{\smash{\big)}69264}$

o. $7\overline{\smash{\big)}16896}$

p. $9\overline{\smash{\big)}50900}$

q. $8\overline{\smash{\big)}67402}$

r. $9\overline{\smash{\big)}87301}$

s. $7\overline{\smash{\big)}10746}$

t. $9\overline{\smash{\big)}74719}$

Exercise D21

a. $10 \overline{\smash{\big)}\ 73462}$

b. $10 \overline{\smash{\big)}\ 64731}$

c. $10 \overline{\smash{\big)}\ 89531}$

d. $10 \overline{\smash{\big)}\ 74416}$

e. $10 \overline{\smash{\big)}\ 84317}$

f. $10 \overline{\smash{\big)}\ 65763}$

g. $10 \overline{\smash{\big)}\ 76417}$

h. $10 \overline{\smash{\big)}\ 96532}$

i. $10 \overline{\smash{\big)}\ 83164}$

j. $10 \overline{\smash{\big)}\ 76532}$

k. $10 \overline{\smash{\big)}\ 63476}$

l. $10 \overline{\smash{\big)}\ 89431}$

m. $10 \overline{\smash{\big)}\ 34762}$

n. $10 \overline{\smash{\big)}\ 80100}$

o. $10 \overline{\smash{\big)}\ 76530}$

p. $10 \overline{\smash{\big)}\ 64010}$

q. $10 \overline{\smash{\big)}\ 67000}$

r. $10 \overline{\smash{\big)}\ 39341}$

s. $10 \overline{\smash{\big)}\ 66427}$

t. $10 \overline{\smash{\big)}\ 61000}$

Exercise D22

a. $11 \overline{) 79641}$

b. $11 \overline{) 99041}$

c. $11 \overline{) 69642}$

d. $11 \overline{) 59694}$

e. $11 \overline{) 39652}$

f. $11 \overline{) 56934}$

g. $11 \overline{) 39654}$

h. $11 \overline{) 49634}$

i. $11 \overline{) 77664}$

j. $11 \overline{) 88894}$

k. $11 \overline{) 79249}$

l. $11 \overline{) 69564}$

m. $11 \overline{) 99079}$

n. $11 \overline{) 89784}$

o. $11 \overline{) 79684}$

p. $11 \overline{) 59764}$

q. $11 \overline{) 79239}$

r. $11 \overline{) 89104}$

s. $11 \overline{) 49506}$

t. $11 \overline{) 77006}$

Exercise D23

a. 12 ⌐85331

b. 12 ⌐74698

c. 12 ⌐63852

d. 12 ⌐97346

e. 12 ⌐99846

f. 12 ⌐79564

g. 12 ⌐89942

h. 12 ⌐78942

i. 12 ⌐55986

j. 12 ⌐86407

k. 12 ⌐74643

l. 12 ⌐58923

m. 12 ⌐16934

n. 12 ⌐29079

o. 12 ⌐86532

p. 12 ⌐89437

q. 12 ⌐84372

r. 12 ⌐36972

s. 12 ⌐48748

t. 12 ⌐96853

Exercise D24

Here is part of the twenty-one times table for you to look at before you go on to the next exercise.

1 x 21 = 21   2 x 21 = 42   3 x 21 = 63

4 x 21 = 84   5 x 21 = 105   6 x 21 = 126

7 x 21 = 147   8 x 21 = 168   9 x 21 = 189

a. 21 ⟌ 2 7 8   b. 21 ⟌ 2 9 8   c. 21 ⟌ 2 3 8

d. 21 ⟌ 2 4 8   e. 21 ⟌ 2 6 9   f. 21 ⟌ 2 8 7

g. 21 ⟌ 2 2 9   h. 21 ⟌ 2 5 0   i. 21 ⟌ 2 7 0

j. 21 ⟌ 2 8 0   k. 21 ⟌ 2 2 0   l. 21 ⟌ 2 7 6

m. 21 ⟌ 2 5 6   n. 21 ⟌ 2 6 1   o. 21 ⟌ 2 9 9

p. 21 ⟌ 2 3 5   q. 21 ⟌ 2 8 9   r. 21 ⟌ 2 4 6

Exercise D25

a. 21 ⟌ 456   b. 21 ⟌ 479   c. 21 ⟌ 497

d. 21 ⟌ 436   e. 21 ⟌ 448   f. 21 ⟌ 469

g. 21 ⟌ 486   h. 21 ⟌ 429   i. 21 ⟌ 450

j. 21 ⟌ 471   k. 21 ⟌ 482   l. 21 ⟌ 421

m. 21 ⟌ 652   n. 21 ⟌ 674   o. 21 ⟌ 699

p. 21 ⟌ 636   q. 21 ⟌ 648   r. 21 ⟌ 669

s. 21 ⟌ 687   t. 21 ⟌ 627   u. 21 ⟌ 650

v. 21 ⟌ 672   w. 21 ⟌ 680   x. 21 ⟌ 685

Exercise D26

a. 21 $\overline{855}$ b. 21 $\overline{874}$ c. 21 $\overline{898}$

d. 21 $\overline{837}$ e. 21 $\overline{847}$ f. 21 $\overline{868}$

g. 21 $\overline{887}$ h. 21 $\overline{829}$ i. 21 $\overline{850}$

j. 21 $\overline{871}$ k. 21 $\overline{885}$ l. 21 $\overline{882}$

m. 21 $\overline{358}$ n. 21 $\overline{378}$ o. 21 $\overline{398}$

p. 21 $\overline{339}$ q. 21 $\overline{346}$ r. 21 $\overline{369}$

s. 21 $\overline{386}$ t. 21 $\overline{324}$ u. 21 $\overline{350}$

v. 21 $\overline{370}$ w. 21 $\overline{380}$ x. 21 $\overline{420}$

Exercise D27

a. 21 ⟌559   b. 21 ⟌597   c. 21 ⟌536

d. 21 ⟌545   e. 21 ⟌568   f. 21 ⟌585

g. 21 ⟌550   h. 21 ⟌573   i. 21 ⟌581

j. 21 ⟌758   k. 21 ⟌778   l. 21 ⟌796

m. 21 ⟌738   n. 21 ⟌745   o. 21 ⟌768

p. 21 ⟌786   q. 21 ⟌751   r. 21 ⟌781

s. 21 ⟌958   t. 21 ⟌979   u. 21 ⟌995

v. 21 ⟌937   w. 21 ⟌968   x. 21 ⟌986

Exercise D28

a. Here is part of the thirty-one times table. Fill in the missing numbers.

1 x 31 = 31   2 x 31 = 62   3 x 31 = ☐

4 x 31 = 124   5 x 31 = ☐   6 x 31 = 186

7 x 31 = ☐   8 x 31 = ☐   9 x 31 = 279

b. 31 ⟌ 3 4 9   c. 31 ⟌ 3 8 7   d. 31 ⟌ 3 9 6

e. 31 ⟌ 3 5 4   f. 31 ⟌ 3 9 0   g. 31 ⟌ 3 7 4

h. 31 ⟌ 3 3 6   i. 31 ⟌ 3 6 4   j. 31 ⟌ 3 8 2

k. 31 ⟌ 6 4 4   l. 31 ⟌ 6 7 5   m. 31 ⟌ 6 5 2

n. 31 ⟌ 6 8 8   o. 31 ⟌ 6 3 5   p. 31 ⟌ 6 6 5

q. 31 ⟌ 6 9 7   r. 31 ⟌ 6 2 3   s. 31 ⟌ 6 9 7

Exercise D29

a. 31 $\overline{)726}$ b. 31 $\overline{)748}$ c. 31 $\overline{)764}$

d. 31 $\overline{)774}$ e. 31 $\overline{)786}$ f. 31 $\overline{)790}$

g. 31 $\overline{)810}$ h. 31 $\overline{)841}$ i. 31 $\overline{)854}$

j. 31 $\overline{)866}$ k. 31 $\overline{)870}$ l. 31 $\overline{)876}$

m. 31 $\overline{)884}$ n. 31 $\overline{)890}$ o. 31 $\overline{)900}$

p. 31 $\overline{)925}$ q. 31 $\overline{)936}$ r. 31 $\overline{)949}$

s. 31 $\overline{)954}$ t. 31 $\overline{)962}$ u. 31 $\overline{)970}$

v. 31 $\overline{)976}$ w. 31 $\overline{)980}$ x. 31 $\overline{)987}$

Exercise D30

a. Here is part of the forty-one times table. Fill in the missing numbers.

1 x 41 = 41   2 x 41 = ☐   3 x 41 = 123

4 x 41 = ☐   5 x 41 = ☐   6 x 41 = 246

7 x 41 = 287   8 x 41 = ☐   9 x 41 = ☐

b. 41 ⟌ 474   **c.** 41 ⟌ 495   **d.** 41 ⟌ 468

e. 41 ⟌ 449   **f.** 41 ⟌ 489   **g.** 41 ⟌ 497

h. 41 ⟌ 490   **i.** 41 ⟌ 465   **j.** 41 ⟌ 498

k. 41 ⟌ 854   **l.** 41 ⟌ 896   **m.** 41 ⟌ 894

n. 41 ⟌ 864   **o.** 41 ⟌ 846   **p.** 41 ⟌ 889

q. 41 ⟌ 897   **r.** 41 ⟌ 842   **s.** 41 ⟌ 876

t. 41 ⟌ 882   **u.** 41 ⟌ 838   **v.** 41 ⟌ 879

Exercise D31

a. Here is part of the fifty-one times table. Fill in the
missing numbers.

1 x 51 = 51   2 x 51 = ☐   3 x 51 = ☐

4 x 51 = 204   5 x 51 = ☐   6 x 51 = ☐

7 x 51 = ☐   8 x 51 = ☐   9 x 51 = ☐

b. 51 ⟌ 5 7 8   **c.** 51 ⟌ 5 8 7   **d.** 51 ⟌ 5 9 8

e. 51 ⟌ 6 5 4   **f.** 51 ⟌ 5 6 9   **g.** 51 ⟌ 6 7 8

h. 51 ⟌ 6 8 9   **i.** 51 ⟌ 7 9 6   **j.** 51 ⟌ 8 8 0

k. 51 ⟌ 9 2 9   **l.** 51 ⟌ 5 3 8   **m.** 51 ⟌ 5 8 6

n. 51 ⟌ 5 9 0   **o.** 51 ⟌ 7 8 4   **p.** 51 ⟌ 8 2 5

q. 51 ⟌ 9 5 6   **r.** 51 ⟌ 8 0 0   **s.** 51 ⟌ 9 0 0

Exercise D32

a. Here is part of the sixty-one times table. Fill in the missing numbers.

$1 \times 61 = \boxed{}$ $2 \times 61 = \boxed{}$ $3 \times 61 = \boxed{}$

$4 \times 61 = \boxed{}$ $5 \times 61 = \boxed{}$ $6 \times 61 = \boxed{}$

$7 \times 61 = 427$ $8 \times 61 = \boxed{}$ $9 \times 61 = \boxed{}$

b. $61 \overline{\smash)689}$ c. $61 \overline{\smash)694}$ d. $61 \overline{\smash)648}$

e. $61 \overline{\smash)746}$ f. $61 \overline{\smash)742}$ g. $61 \overline{\smash)849}$

h. $61 \overline{\smash)859}$ i. $61 \overline{\smash)959}$ j. $61 \overline{\smash)984}$

k. $61 \overline{\smash)992}$ l. $61 \overline{\smash)900}$ m. $61 \overline{\smash)798}$

n. $61 \overline{\smash)800}$ o. $61 \overline{\smash)930}$ p. $61 \overline{\smash)700}$

Exercise D33

a. Here is part of the seventy-one times table. Fill in the missing numbers.

1 x 71 = ☐   2 x 71 = ☐   3 x 71 = 213

4 x 71 = ☐   5 x 71 = ☐   6 x 71 = ☐

7 x 71 = ☐   8 x 71 = 568   9 x 71 = ☐

b. 71 ⟌ 7 8 7   **c.** 71 ⟌ 8 5 8   **d.** 71 ⟌ 7 8 0

e. 71 ⟌ 8 0 4   **f.** 71 ⟌ 7 9 6   **g.** 71 ⟌ 8 9 0

h. 71 ⟌ 8 9 9   **i.** 71 ⟌ 9 4 2   **j.** 71 ⟌ 9 5 3

k. 71 ⟌ 9 7 8   **l.** 71 ⟌ 9 9 9   **m.** 71 ⟌ 8 8 0

n. 71 ⟌ 8 6 1   **o.** 71 ⟌ 8 2 6   **p.** 71 ⟌ 7 6 1

Exercise D34

a. Here is part of the eighty-one times table. Fill in the missing numbers.

1 x 81 = ☐   2 x 81 = ☐   3 x 81 = ☐

4 x 81 = 324   5 x 81 = ☐   6 x 81 = ☐

7 x 81 = ☐   8 x 81 = ☐   9 x 81 = ☐

b. 81 ⟌ 897   c. 81 ⟌ 899   d. 81 ⟌ 880

e. 81 ⟌ 904   f. 81 ⟌ 908   g. 81 ⟌ 986

h. 81 ⟌ 999   i. 81 ⟌ 900   j. 81 ⟌ 946

k. 81 ⟌ 917   l. 81 ⟌ 972   m. 81 ⟌ 961

n. 81 ⟌ 928   o. 81 ⟌ 942   p. 81 ⟌ 935

Exercise D35

a. Complete the table.

$1 \times 32 = \boxed{}$ $2 \times 32 = \boxed{}$ $3 \times 32 = 96$

$4 \times 32 = \boxed{}$ $5 \times 32 = \boxed{}$ $6 \times 32 = \boxed{}$

$7 \times 32 = \boxed{}$ $8 \times 32 = 256$ $9 \times 32 = \boxed{}$

b. $32\,\overline{)369}$ **c.** $32\,\overline{)378}$ **d.** $32\,\overline{)389}$

e. $32\,\overline{)698}$ **f.** $32\,\overline{)650}$ **g.** $32\,\overline{)678}$

h. $32\,\overline{)669}$ **i.** $32\,\overline{)749}$ **j.** $32\,\overline{)768}$

k. $32\,\overline{)777}$ **l.** $32\,\overline{)564}$ **m.** $32\,\overline{)647}$

n. $32\,\overline{)586}$ **o.** $32\,\overline{)457}$ **p.** $32\,\overline{)546}$

Exercise D36

a. Complete the table.

1 x 42 = ☐   2 x 42 = ☐   3 x 42 = ☐

4 x 42 = 168   5 x 42 = ☐   6 x 42 = ☐

7 x 42 = ☐   8 x 42 = ☐   9 x 42 = 378

b. 42 ⟌ 479   **c.** 42 ⟌ 487   **d.** 42 ⟌ 499

e. 42 ⟌ 518   **f.** 42 ⟌ 564   **g.** 42 ⟌ 589

h. 42 ⟌ 609   **i.** 42 ⟌ 715   **j.** 42 ⟌ 868

k. 42 ⟌ 906   **l.** 42 ⟌ 857   **m.** 42 ⟌ 430

n. 42 ⟌ 799   **o.** 42 ⟌ 600   **p.** 42 ⟌ 800

Exercise D37

a. Complete the table.

1 x 52 = ☐   2 x 52 = 104   3 x 52 = ☐

4 x 52 = ☐   5 x 52 = ☐   6 x 52 = ☐

7 x 52 = 364   8 x 52 = ☐   9 x 52 = ☐

b. 52 ⟌ 5 7 9   **c.** 52 ⟌ 5 9 0   **d.** 52 ⟌ 6 0 0

e. 52 ⟌ 6 2 8   **f.** 52 ⟌ 6 7 9   **g.** 52 ⟌ 7 2 9

h. 52 ⟌ 7 8 9   **i.** 52 ⟌ 7 9 0   **j.** 52 ⟌ 8 9 6

k. 52 ⟌ 9 5 7   **l.** 52 ⟌ 9 8 7   **m.** 52 ⟌ 6 8 8

n. 52 ⟌ 8 0 0   **o.** 52 ⟌ 9 0 0   **p.** 52 ⟌ 7 0 0

Exercise D38

a. Complete the table.

1 x 62 = ☐   2 x 62 = ☐   3 x 62 = 186

4 x 62 = ☐   5 x 62 = ☐   6 x 62 = ☐

7 x 62 = 434   8 x 62 = ☐   9 x 62 = ☐

b. 62 ⟌ 6 8 7   c. 62 ⟌ 6 9 0   d. 62 ⟌ 7 0 4

e. 62 ⟌ 7 3 4   f. 62 ⟌ 7 5 6   g. 62 ⟌ 7 9 9

h. 62 ⟌ 8 3 7   i. 62 ⟌ 8 7 6   j. 62 ⟌ 9 0 0

k. 62 ⟌ 9 7 6   l. 62 ⟌ 9 9 9   m. 62 ⟌ 6 3 4

n. 62 ⟌ 8 2 0   o. 62 ⟌ 8 9 0   p. 62 ⟌ 9 4 0

Exercise D39

a. Complete the table.

1 x 72 = ☐   2 x 72 = ☐   3 x 72 = ☐

4 x 72 = ☐   5 x 72 = 360   6 x 72 = ☐

7 x 72 = ☐   8 x 72 = ☐   9 x 72 = 648

b. 72 ⌐794   **c.** 72 ⌐806   **d.** 72 ⌐829

e. 72 ⌐894   **f.** 72 ⌐910   **g.** 72 ⌐998

h. 72 ⌐904   **i.** 72 ⌐962   **j.** 72 ⌐959

k. 72 ⌐991   **l.** 72 ⌐716   **m.** 72 ⌐746

n. 72 ⌐864   **o.** 72 ⌐880   **p.** 72 ⌐874

Exercise D40

a. Complete the table.

1 x 82 = [　　]   2 x 82 = [　　]   3 x 82 = [　　]

4 x 82 = [　　]   5 x 82 = 410   6 x 82 = [　　]

7 x 82 = [　　]   8 x 82 = [　　]   9 x 82 = [　　]

b. 82 ⟌ 9 0 6   c. 82 ⟌ 9 4 3   d. 82 ⟌ 9 5 4

e. 82 ⟌ 9 2 9   f. 82 ⟌ 9 9 0   g. 82 ⟌ 9 3 7

h. 82 ⟌ 9 9 9   i. 82 ⟌ 9 1 9   j. 82 ⟌ 8 8 0

k. 82 ⟌ 1 0 6 4   l. 82 ⟌ 1 1 9 4   m. 82 ⟌ 1 6 9 4

n. 82 ⟌ 2 6 9 4   o. 82 ⟌ 3 7 8 2   p. 82 ⟌ 4 9 2 4

Exercise D41

a. Complete the table.

1 x 43 = ☐   2 x 43 = ☐   3 x 43 = 129

4 x 43 = ☐   5 x 43 = ☐   6 x 43 = ☐

7 x 43 = 301   8 x 43 = ☐   9 x 43 = ☐

b. 43 ⟌ 4 7 6   c. 43 ⟌ 4 9 8   d. 43 ⟌ 5 6 4

e. 43 ⟌ 6 4 7   f. 43 ⟌ 7 6 5   g. 43 ⟌ 7 9 9

h. 43 ⟌ 8 4 6   i. 43 ⟌ 8 9 8   j. 43 ⟌ 9 4 6

k. 43 ⟌ 8 7 6   l. 43 ⟌ 8 9 4   m. 43 ⟌ 8 8 9

n. 43 ⟌ 4 4 6   o. 43 ⟌ 5 0 0   p. 43 ⟌ 5 4 2

Exercise D42

a. Complete the table.

1 x 54 = ☐   2 x 54 = 108   3 x 54 = ☐
4 x 54 = ☐   5 x 54 = ☐   6 x 54 = ☐
7 x 54 = 378   8 x 54 = ☐   9 x 54 = ☐

b. 54 ⟌ 5 9 9   **c.** 54 ⟌ 8 6 0   **d.** 54 ⟌ 6 0 4

e. 54 ⟌ 8 0 1   **f.** 54 ⟌ 6 9 4   **g.** 54 ⟌ 7 8 9

h. 54 ⟌ 8 9 4   **i.** 54 ⟌ 9 0 4   **j.** 54 ⟌ 9 4 6

k. 54 ⟌ 9 8 9   **l.** 54 ⟌ 9 3 0   **m.** 54 ⟌ 6 5 1

n. 54 ⟌ 1 0 9 4   **o.** 54 ⟌ 1 1 8 6   **p.** 54 ⟌ 1 3 8 7

Exercise D43

a. Complete the table.

1 x 65 = ☐ 2 x 65 = ☐ 3 x 65 = ☐

4 x 65 = ☐ 5 x 65 = ☐ 6 x 65 = ☐

7 x 65 = ☐ 8 x 65 = 520 9 x 65 = ☐

b. 65 ⟌ 7 5 4   c. 65 ⟌ 8 0 0   d. 65 ⟌ 8 6 3

e. 65 ⟌ 9 0 0   f. 65 ⟌ 9 2 4   g. 65 ⟌ 9 5 6

h. 65 ⟌ 9 7 6   i. 65 ⟌ 9 8 0   j. 65 ⟌ 9 9 9

k. 65 ⟌ 6 9 4   l. 65 ⟌ 7 0 0   m. 65 ⟌ 7 4 0

n. 65 ⟌ 8 3 1   o. 65 ⟌ 1 2 4 0   p. 65 ⟌ 1 3 0 6

Exercise D44

a. Complete the table.

1 x 75 = ☐   2 x 75 = ☐   3 x 75 = ☐

4 x 75 = 300   5 x 75 = ☐   6 x 75 = ☐

7 x 75 = ☐   8 x 75 = ☐   9 x 75 = ☐

b. 7 5 $\overline{)854}$ c. 7 5 $\overline{)942}$ d. 7 5 $\overline{)794}$

e. 7 5 $\overline{)800}$ f. 7 5 $\overline{)882}$ g. 7 5 $\overline{)898}$

h. 7 5 $\overline{)901}$ i. 7 5 $\overline{)945}$ j. 7 5 $\overline{)978}$

k. 7 5 $\overline{)760}$ l. 7 5 $\overline{)850}$ m. 7 5 $\overline{)931}$

n. 7 5 $\overline{)998}$ o. 7 5 $\overline{)1426}$ p. 7 5 $\overline{)1542}$

Exercise D45

a. Complete the table.

1 x 87 = ☐   2 x 87 = 174   3 x 87 = ☐

4 x 87 = ☐   5 x 87 = ☐   6 x 87 = 522

7 x 87 = 609   8 x 87 = ☐   9 x 87 = ☐

b. 87 ⟌ 9 8 4   **c.** 87 ⟌ 9 9 8   **d.** 87 ⟌ 8 8 4

e. 87 ⟌ 8 9 2   **f.** 87 ⟌ 1 0 4 6   **g.** 87 ⟌ 1 4 6 8

h. 87 ⟌ 1 9 6 4   **i.** 87 ⟌ 2 6 4 2   **j.** 87 ⟌ 3 6 8 4

k. 87 ⟌ 7 6 4 2   **l.** 87 ⟌ 5 4 9 3   **m.** 87 ⟌ 6 6 4 2

n. 87 ⟌ 7 8 6 4   **o.** 87 ⟌ 8 9 4 3   **p.** 87 ⟌ 9 0 0 0

Exercise D46

a. Complete the table.

1 x 98 = ☐   2 x 98 = ☐   3 x 98 = 294

4 x 98 = ☐   5 x 98 = ☐   6 x 98 = ☐

7 x 98 = 686   8 x 98 = 784   9 x 98 = ☐

b. 98 ⟌ 1 0 9 4   **c.** 98 ⟌ 9 8 2   **d.** 98 ⟌ 4 5 4 2

e. 98 ⟌ 1 1 6 4   **f.** 98 ⟌ 2 1 6 2   **g.** 98 ⟌ 1 9 8 4

h. 98 ⟌ 3 8 7 4   **i.** 98 ⟌ 5 6 4 2   **j.** 98 ⟌ 7 6 4 2

k. 98 ⟌ 8 5 4 2   **l.** 98 ⟌ 9 6 0 4   **m.** 98 ⟌ 9 8 1 1

n. 98 ⟌ 9 9 1 6   **o.** 98 ⟌ 6 9 4 7   **p.** 98 ⟌ 3 5 6 4

Exercise D47

a. Complete the table.

1 x 45 = ☐   2 x 45 = 90   3 x 45 = ☐

4 x 45 = 180   5 x 45 = ☐   6 x 45 = ☐

7 x 45 = ☐   8 x 45 = ☐   9 x 45 = 405

b. 45 ⟌ 5 0 6 4   **c.** 45 ⟌ 4 9 4 0   **d.** 45 ⟌ 5 4 6 2

e. 45 ⟌ 6 4 2 7   **f.** 45 ⟌ 7 6 4 2   **g.** 45 ⟌ 8 1 6 2

h. 45 ⟌ 8 5 3 4   **i.** 45 ⟌ 9 7 6 2   **j.** 45 ⟌ 9 4 1 6

k. 45 ⟌ 9 3 4 6   **l.** 45 ⟌ 9 4 6 2   **m.** 45 ⟌ 9 1 0 6

n. 45 ⟌ 9 2 3 7   **o.** 45 ⟌ 4 7 0 6   **p.** 45 ⟌ 5 0 6 4

Exercise D48

a. Complete the table.

$1 \times 56 = 56$ $2 \times 56 = \boxed{}$ $3 \times 56 = \boxed{}$

$4 \times 56 = \boxed{}$ $5 \times 56 = 280$ $6 \times 56 = \boxed{}$

$7 \times 56 = \boxed{}$ $8 \times 56 = \boxed{}$ $9 \times 56 = 504$

b. $56 \overline{\smash{\big)}\ 6294}$ **c.** $56 \overline{\smash{\big)}\ 7384}$ **d.** $56 \overline{\smash{\big)}\ 5946}$

e. $56 \overline{\smash{\big)}\ 7426}$ **f.** $56 \overline{\smash{\big)}\ 8464}$ **g.** $56 \overline{\smash{\big)}\ 8992}$

h. $56 \overline{\smash{\big)}\ 5708}$ **i.** $56 \overline{\smash{\big)}\ 5927}$ **j.** $56 \overline{\smash{\big)}\ 6046}$

k. $56 \overline{\smash{\big)}\ 6178}$ **l.** $56 \overline{\smash{\big)}\ 4630}$ **m.** $56 \overline{\smash{\big)}\ 4213}$

n. $56 \overline{\smash{\big)}\ 5056}$ **o.** $56 \overline{\smash{\big)}\ 2859}$ **p.** $56 \overline{\smash{\big)}\ 2349}$

Exercise D49

a. Complete the table.

1 x 67 = [ ]　　2 x 67 = [ ]　　3 x 67 = 201

4 x 67 = 268　　5 x 67 = [ ]　　6 x 67 = [ ]

7 x 67 = [ ]　　8 x 67 = 536　　9 x 67 = [ ]

b. 6 7 ⟌ 7 3 9 4　　**c.** 6 7 ⟌ 8 4 4 2　　**d.** 6 7 ⟌ 9 2 8 4

e. 6 7 ⟌ 9 7 4 2　　**f.** 6 7 ⟌ 6 9 3 4　　**g.** 6 7 ⟌ 9 9 4 2

h. 6 7 ⟌ 1 6 7 4　　**i.** 6 7 ⟌ 2 4 6 4　　**j.** 6 7 ⟌ 2 0 4 6

k. 6 7 ⟌ 2 8 7 4　　**l.** 6 7 ⟌ 4 9 6 4　　**m.** 6 7 ⟌ 6 8 0 4

n. 6 7 ⟌ 5 3 7 6　　**o.** 6 7 ⟌ 2 0 7 9　　**p.** 6 7 ⟌ 2 6 9 4

Exercise D50

a. Complete the table.

1 x 78 = ☐   2 x 78 = ☐   3 x 78 = ☐

4 x 78 = 312   5 x 78 = ☐   6 x 78 = ☐

7 x 78 = ☐   8 x 78 = ☐   9 x 78 = 702

b. 78 ⟌ 8 7 4 2   **c.** 78 ⟌ 9 1 6 4   **d.** 78 ⟌ 8 9 6 4

e. 78 ⟌ 1 0 4 4   **f.** 78 ⟌ 2 6 4 3   **g.** 78 ⟌ 5 4 6 4

h. 78 ⟌ 6 3 4 2   **i.** 78 ⟌ 7 9 2 4   **j.** 78 ⟌ 8 0 4 6

k. 78 ⟌ 8 4 7 3   **l.** 78 ⟌ 8 8 4 4   **m.** 78 ⟌ 9 0 0 4

n. 78 ⟌ 9 2 0 6   **o.** 78 ⟌ 7 0 4 3   **p.** 78 ⟌ 7 8 1 7

Exercise D51

a. Complete the table.

1 x 89 = ☐   2 x 89 = 178   3 x 89 = ☐

4 x 89 = ☐   5 x 89 = ☐   6 x 89 = ☐

7 x 89 = 623   8 x 89 = ☐   9 x 89 = 801

b. 89 ⟌ 9 9 4 2   **c.** 89 ⟌ 9 9 8 9   **d.** 89 ⟌ 9 7 9 0

e. 89 ⟌ 7 4 2 6   **f.** 89 ⟌ 6 3 0 4   **g.** 89 ⟌ 6 8 0 1

h. 89 ⟌ 5 2 4 1   **i.** 89 ⟌ 1 7 9 1   **j.** 89 ⟌ 2 3 4 6

k. 89 ⟌ 4 4 5 6   **l.** 89 ⟌ 5 3 6 7   **m.** 89 ⟌ 8 0 2 0

n. 89 ⟌ 6 2 4 7   **o.** 89 ⟌ 8 9 0 9   **p.** 89 ⟌ 4 4 6 2

Exercise D52

Another way of writing $6\overline{)372}$ with quotient 62 is $372 \div 6 = 62$

Or $504 \div 7 = 72$ is $7\overline{)504}$ with quotient 72

Write these examples in the other form, and find the answers.

a. $5\overline{)665}$ b. $8\overline{)976}$ c. $4\overline{)520}$

d. $2\overline{)702}$ e. $3\overline{)852}$ f. $7\overline{)854}$

g. $9\overline{)918}$ h. $10\overline{)130}$ i. $3\overline{)492}$

j. $6\overline{)612}$ k. $5\overline{)755}$ l. $2\overline{)332}$

m. $7\overline{)434}$ n. $9\overline{)198}$ o. $3\overline{)732}$

Exercise D53

$$\frac{122\text{R}.3}{7\overline{)857}} \qquad \text{may be written} \quad 857 \div 7 = 122\text{R}.3$$

$$\frac{127\text{R}.3}{6\overline{)765}} \qquad \text{may be written} \quad 765 \div 6 = 127\text{R}.3$$

$$894 \div 7 = 129\text{R}.5 \quad \text{may be written} \quad 7\overline{)894}^{\,129\text{R}.5}$$

$$766 \div 5 = 153\text{R}.1 \quad \text{may be written} \quad 5\overline{)766}^{\,153\text{R}.1}$$

Work these examples and write them the other way.

a. $674 \div 5 =$ 　　　　　　　　**b.** $7\overline{)999}$

c. $6\overline{)894}$ 　　　　　　　　**d.** $811 \div 8 =$

e. $729 \div 8 =$ 　　　　　　　　**f.** $5\overline{)527}$

g. $4\overline{)921}$ 　　　　　　　　**h.** $601 \div 5 =$

Exercise D54

a. 10 ÷ 2 =

b. 25 ÷ 5 =

c. 14 ÷ 7 =

d. 9 ÷ 3 =

e. 8 ÷ 4 =

f. 18 ÷ 6 =

g. 20 ÷ 4 =

h. 27 ÷ 9 =

i. 32 ÷ 2 =

j. 44 ÷ 11 =

k. 56 ÷ 7 =

l. 3 ÷ 1 =

m. 36 ÷ 9 =

n. 49 ÷ 7 =

o. 30 ÷ 2 =

p. 18 ÷ 3 =

q. 22 ÷ 2 =

r. 45 ÷ 9 =

s. 24 ÷ 6 =

t. 16 ÷ 4 =

u. 60 ÷ 12 =

v. 72 ÷ 6 =

w. 45 ÷ 9 =

x. 28 ÷ 7 =

y. 55 ÷ 11 =

z. 20 ÷ 10 =

Exercise D55

a. Share twelve equally amongst three.

b. How many times can three be taken from nine?

c. How many nuts can each of four boys have from sixteen?

d. Twelve divided by two.

e. Two postage stamps cost thirty-two pence. What does one cost?

f. Divide twenty-one by seven.

g. At three km per hour, how long does it take to walk nine kilometres?

h. What is one half of twenty-four?

i. What is one third of eighteen?

Exercise D56

a. Nine divided by three.

b. Sixty divided by ten.

c. Ten pence is shared equally between two brothers. How much does each receive?

d. Sixteen divided by four.

e. Three sisters have equal shares of 30p. How much does each receive?

f. Eighteen divided by six.

g. Fourteen divided by two.

h. One hour has sixty minutes. How many minutes are there in half an hour?

i. My sister's wages are £40 a week. She gives half to my mother. How much is that?

j. Twenty-four divided by three.

k. My mother has made ten iced buns. The five members of the family have equal shares. How many buns does each of us have?

Exercise D57

a. Share twenty-eight by seven.

b. In four weeks I saved ninety-six pence. How much is that per week?

c. How many times can seven be taken from twenty-one?

d. Two numbers multiplied together make twenty-five. One is five. What is the other?

e. Two weeks' pocket money is eighty-six pence. What is one week's pocket money?

f. How many children can have five pence out of forty-five pence.

g. Eighteen divided by three.

h. Share thirty-two fruits amongst four boys.

i. In our garden are forty-eight cabbage plants arranged in six rows. How many is that per row?

j. Mother bought six lbs of sprouts for seventy-two pence. How much per lb is this?

Exercise D58

a. A class of 36 children is divided into 6 equal groups. How many will there be in each group?

b. How many times can I take 7 from 35?

c. How many are left over when I have given 5 sweets to each of nine children, out of 48 sweets?

d. A boy is sponsored for a walk at 8p a kilometre. He receives 64p. How many kilometres did he walk?

e. Each child in the class sold 4 programmes for our sport's day. 96 programmes were sold in all. How many children in the class?

f. A car did 125 kilometres on 5 gallons of petrol. How many kilometres per gallon was that?

g. At 9p a copy, how many booklets could I obtain for 108p?

h. What is the remainder when 146 is shared by 10?

Exercise D59

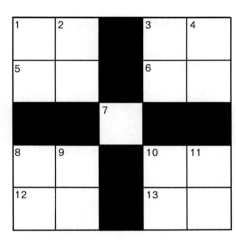

Across

1. 96 ÷ 8
3. 45 ÷ 3
5. 120 ÷ 4
6. 66 ÷ 3
7. 81 ÷ 9
8. 110 ÷ 10
10. 93 ÷ 3
12. 180 ÷ 3
13. 48 ÷ 2

Down

1. 26 ÷ 2
2. 60 ÷ 3
3. 60 ÷ 5
4. 104 ÷ 2
8. 48 ÷ 3
9. 100 ÷ 10
10. 64 ÷ 2
11. 42 ÷ 3

Exercise D60

Across

1. 990 ÷ 9
5. 54 ÷ 2
6. 30 ÷ 2
8. 1000 ÷ 2

Down

2. 34 ÷ 2
3. 250 ÷ 2
4. 1000 ÷ 4
7. 120 ÷ 3

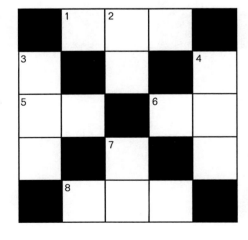

Exercise D61

1	2		3		4		5
	6				7	8	
9			10				
		11			12		
13	14						
			15	16		17	
18		19		20			
						21	

Across

1. $48 \div 4$
6. $500 \div 5$
7. $262 \div 2$
9. $36 \div 3$
10. $160 \div 2$
12. $212 \div 2$
13. $256 \div 2$
15. $63 \div 3$
17. $160 \div 4$
18. $412 \div 2$
20. $1000 \div 2$
21. $100 \div 4$

Down

2. $424 \div 2$
3. $324 \div 3$
4. $84 \div 4$
5. $55 \div 5$
8. $700 \div 2$
11. $54 \div 3$
12. $60 \div 4$
14. $600 \div 3$
16. $300 \div 2$
17. $804 \div 2$
18. $66 \div 3$
19. $126 \div 2$

Exercise D62

Across

2.	30 ÷ 2	14.	42 ÷ 2
3.	232 ÷ 2	16.	639 ÷ 3
5.	345 ÷ 3	18.	430 ÷ 2
7.	40 ÷ 2	20.	60 ÷ 5
8.	369 ÷ 3	22.	800 ÷ 2
10.	624 ÷ 2	23.	375 ÷ 3
12.	69 ÷ 3	24.	48 ÷ 2

Down

1.	336 ÷ 3	11.	500 ÷ 4
2.	32 ÷ 2	13.	72 ÷ 2
4.	309 ÷ 3	15.	480 ÷ 4
5.	48 ÷ 4	17.	624 ÷ 2
6.	264 ÷ 2	19.	50 ÷ 5
8.	363 ÷ 3	21.	500 ÷ 2
9.	88 ÷ 4	23.	28 ÷ 2

Enjoy Mathematics

The complete series consists of six books, as follows:

Book 1   **Basic Addition** 1-871044-15-4

Book 2   **Basic Subtraction** 1-871044-20-0

Book 3   **Basic Multiplication** 1-871044-05-7

Book 4   **Basic Division** 1-871044-10-3

Book 5   **Revision Exercises and Puzzles** 1-871044-25-1

Book 6   **Answer Book** 1-871044-30-8

We hope that you have enjoyed using this book, and that you
have found it helpful.

If you would like to order other books in this series, they can be
purchased directly from the publisher.

To order over the phone using a credit or debit card, call:

01733 898105

Order online by visiting our website:

www.forwardpress.co.uk

If you have any questions about this book, or any other books in
the Enjoy Mathematics series, you can email us:

Info@forwardpress.co.uk

Thank you